Discovering Mission San Antonio de Padua

BY ZACHARY ANDERSON

Cavendish Square

New York

Published in 2015 by Cavendish Square Publishing, LLC
243 5th Avenue, Suite 136, New York, NY 10016

CPSIA Compliance Information: Batch #WS14CSQ

All websites were available and accurate when this book was sent to press.

Library of Congress Cataloging-in-Publication Data

Anderson, Zachary.
Discovering Mission San Antonio de Padua / Zachary Anderson.
pages cm. — (California missions)
Includes index.
ISBN 978-1-62713-082-0 (hardcover) ISBN 978-1-62713-084-4 (ebook)
1. San Antonio de Pádua (Mission)—History—Juvenile literature. 2. Spanish mission buildings—California—King City Region—History—Juvenile literature. 3. Franciscans—California—King City Region—History—Juvenile literature. 4. Salinan Indians—Missions—California—King City Region—History—Juvenile literature. 5. California—History—To 1846—Juvenile literature. I. Title.
F869.S175A55 2015
979.4'85—dc23
2014006688

Editorial Director: Dean Miller
Editor: Kristen Susienka
Copy Editor: Cynthia Roby
Art Director: Jeffrey Talbot
Designer: Douglas Brooks
Photo Researcher: J8 Media
Production Manager: Jennifer Ryder-Talbot
Production Editor: David McNamara

Printed in the United States of America

Contents

Founded in 1771, Mission San Antonio de Padua was third of the California missions.

1
The Spanish in California

THE SPANISH COME TO ALTA CALIFORNIA

Stretching along California's coast, from San Diego to San Francisco, stand twenty-one Spanish missions. These religious communities, set up between 1769 and 1823, brought Spanish people from Mexico (then called New Spain) to California (known then as *Alta*, or "upper," California). It was there that many belonging to the area's Native tribes were baptized and taught Spanish language and culture. The key to unlock much of California's rich history can be found in these settlements.

Today Mission San Antonio de Padua stands proudly against California's rolling hills as a symbol of a time of change and challenge for the Spanish and the Native Californians. San Antonio de Padua was the third mission founded (July 14, 1771) by Junípero Serra, a **Franciscan friar**, or *fray* in Spanish. From its beginning, Mission San Antonio de Padua had a unique and interesting story.

THE SPANISH ARRIVE

In 1492, Italian explorer Christopher Columbus was sent on a voyage west by the Spanish king and queen for whom he worked.

Christopher Columbus's arrival in the New World in 1492 signaled a turning point in the history of Spain and the rest of the world.

His mission was to find a water route from Europe to Asia. This was during a time when many countries were exploring the seas, hoping to find riches and new land. Columbus's trip brought him accidentally to the Americas (North America, South America, and Central America), and from that moment he positioned Spain to claim its land. The king of Spain was first interested in this land because he believed that explorers might find a river that flowed across the entire continent, toward Asia. Many tried, and all failed.

One of the Spanish **conquistadors** who followed the route after Columbus was Hernán Cortés. In 1519, Cortés sailed to present-day Mexico, where he encountered a rich and powerful Native tribe called the Aztecs. In 1521, Cortés and his men conquered the Aztecs, taking all of their lands and renaming the area New Spain.

In 1542, Spanish explorer Juan Rodríguez Cabrillo was sent by the Spanish government to investigate the California coastline. Although he sailed past much of California's coast, Cabrillo found no water route through America and no riches. Cabrillo died before the trip's end, but he is considered one of the first Europeans to explore the West Coast by ship.

In 1596, Sebastián Vizcaíno was sent by the Spanish to Alta California to secure some ports along the coast. In 1602, Vizcaíno and his men established the port of Monterey, which he named in honor of the **viceroy** of New Spain, Don Gaspár de Zúñiga y Acevedo, the Count of Monte Rey. He also established the port of San Diego. However, as this expedition also did not lead to treasures and a new route to Asia, the Spanish would abandon that part of California for the next 160 years.

Throughout the 1500s, 1600s, and 1700s, Spanish explorers toured the new country and claimed more land for Spain.

2
The Salinan People

LIVING OFF THE LAND

Before the Europeans arrived, the land in the area we now consider California was already populated by many different groups of **indigenous** people. About 2,000 to 3,000 people of the Salinan tribe inhabited the region where San Antonio de Padua was built. Today there is little known about the ancient Salinan people. Even the original name of their tribe is not known. They are called "Salinan" because of the geographic area where they originated: near the Salinas River.

What is known is that the Salinan people lived off the plants and animals in their environment. They ate fish, reptiles, birds, and other small animals. The men in the tribe hunted these animals with bows and arrows made from wood, stone, and animal hides. Some animals, though, could not be killed or eaten. These animals were sacred.

California bears many different types of plants that can be eaten. The people gathered acorns, grass, berries, and even prickly pears. The women in the tribe made a mush from the acorns by grinding and then cooking them. The Salinan ate this oatmeal-like food with their hands. Sometimes they baked acorn breads using the ground acorn flour. Since raw acorns are bitter, though, they had to be careful to clean the acorns before eating them. They did this by washing the acorn flour ten times with water.

CLOTHING

The Salinan people also made whatever clothing they wore out of animal hides. Because the summers were so hot, men and children often wore nothing. Women wore an apron with a front and back, and a fringe cut into the bottom. These skirts were usually

Before and during the mission era, Native women often did the cooking using tools around them.

made from tree bark that was strung onto a cord. Another item of clothing women tended to wear was a cap that looked like a basket. These caps helped them carry heavy loads on their heads. During the winter, the Salinan wore robes or blankets, made from the skins of deer, wildcat, and sea otter, to keep warm. The Salinan usually did not wear shoes and often decorated themselves with ear ornaments or red and yellow body paint.

RELIGIOUS BELIEFS AND PRACTICES

Before the missionaries came to California, the Salinan practiced their own religion. They believed in a Creator and that all things had life. They also had advisors, called shamans, whom they believed could communicate with the gods. In the Salinan tribe, shamans were usually men. There could be several shamans in a tribe. One might be a weather shaman, who the people believed could control the weather. Another might be in charge of curing the sick.

LANGUAGE

The language of the Salinan people is called "Hokan." According to the Salinan tribe today, it is the oldest-known language in California. Much of the words and phrases have been passed down through generations, and today these are spoken among the Salinan descendants. There were different **dialects** of the language spoken in the areas where Salinan tribes lived. While the languages varied slightly in sound, they were similar enough that all Salianans could understand each other and communicate.

TRADING AND OTHER NATIVE GROUPS

The Salinan had neighboring tribes on three sides. To the east were the Yokuts, who were friendly. The Yokuts traded goods as well as information, knowledge, and traditions with the Salinan people. To the north were the Ohlone people, also known as the Costanoan tribe, who did not get along with the Salinan. As a result, the two often fought. To the south were the Chumash, who were separated from the Salinan by mountains, thus the two rarely interacted.

When the Spanish arrived in California, the lifestyle of the Salinan changed forever. There are very few members of this tribe left today, and much of their culture was lost as a result of the mission system.

The arrival of the Spanish signaled big changes for the Salinan people living in the area.

3
The
Mission System

THE MISSIONS UNDER FRANCISCANS

The mission system had been set up in the 1600s throughout *Baja*, or "lower," California, to **convert** the Native people in the area to **Christianity**. All missions were originally led by the Jesuit order of priests. However, in the 1760s, Spain worried that the Jesuits were becoming too powerful, and thereby ordered the Jesuits to leave. The Jesuits were then replaced by Franciscan friars. The men of the Franciscan order would start and run the twenty-one missions of Alta California.

The mission system under the Franciscans was different from that of the Jesuits. Instead of just sending religious missionaries, the Spanish government sent both soldiers and friars to live in Alta California. The soldiers were there to enforce rules and keep the peace, while the friars taught the indigenous people about Christianity and turned them into Spanish citizens. Any Native Californian who converted to Christianity and came to live at the mission was called a **neophyte**. The missionaries' role was to attract them to the missions. There they would teach them Spanish ways of farming and work methods. This would prepare them to assist in building the mission structures as well as farm the land. The friars never forgot that the land belonged to the Native people. They planned to return it to the neophytes once they had become Spanish citizens. This process of transferring control of the mission away from the church is called **secularization**.

WHY THE MISSIONS WERE BUILT

There were several ideas behind the mission system. Religion was one of these ideas. During the time that Spain started founding the missions, it was largely a Catholic country. This means that the Spanish people followed the teachings of **Catholicism**, which

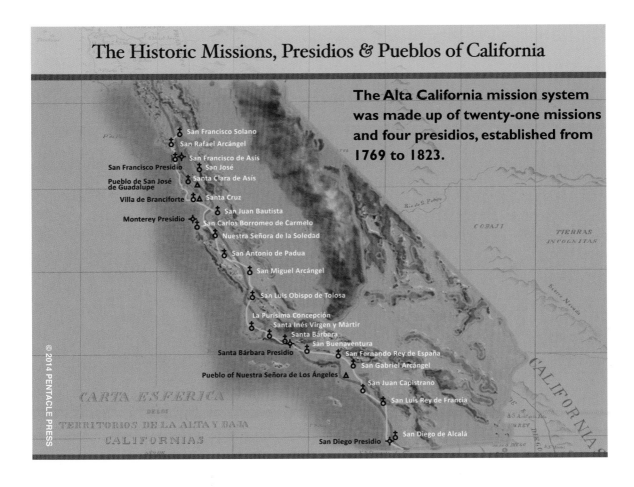

The Historic Missions, Presidios & Pueblos of California

The Alta California mission system was made up of twenty-one missions and four presidios, established from 1769 to 1823.

is a denomination, or type, of Christianity. Missionaries wanted to spread Christianity to people in other countries.

There was also a political reason for starting the missions. In the 1700s, countries such as Russia and England began building forts and claiming land in the northern parts of Alta California. Spain saw these countries as a threat and set up the missions and *presidios*, or forts, to expand their empire and force many of the Native people to learn the Spanish language.

HOW THE MISSIONS AFFECTED THE NATIVE PEOPLE

At the time the mission system was established, many Europeans assumed that the First People of California were unsophisticated. The Native people had their own ways of making a life on the land, their own languages, and their own moral and spiritual beliefs. We know today that their civilization was different from the European way of life, but it was just as cultured and valuable.

Missions such as San Antonio de Padua were permanent structures where friars could teach Native people Christianity and how to be like the Spanish.

4
The Founding of the Mission

SPAIN'S PLAN FOR CALIFORNIA

The Spanish government planned to establish a chain of missions along the coast of California, from San Diego up toward what is now northern California. This trail would make it more difficult for countries such as England and Russia, also interested in the land, to try to take over. It would also mean that the missions were close to Native populations, and that those Native people who converted would become Spanish citizens. San Antonio de Padua was the third of these missions, established on July 14, 1771.

The Spanish government sent two Franciscan friars and several soldiers to found each mission. Each mission was given $1,000 in Spanish money to pay for supplies. When the Jesuits were told to leave the missions in the 1760s, an army captain named Gaspár de Portolá was made the governor of both Baja California and Alta California. In 1769, he led an expedition to New Spain to set up the first mission and claim land for Spain.

Fray Junípero Serra traveled with soldiers to find each mission, which he dedicated with a religious ceremony called a Mass.

JUNÍPERO SERRA AND THE FIRST MISSION

Accompanying Portolá on this expedition was a Franciscan friar named Junípero Serra. Serra would become the most important figure in the founding of the Alta California missions.

Junípero Serra was born Miguel José Serra on the island of Majorca, Spain, on November 24, 1713. Serra knew he wanted to be a priest at a young age, so at sixteen he took his vows to join the Franciscans. When a young man becomes a Franciscan, he chooses a new name for himself. Serra chose the name Junípero in honor of a close friend and follower of Saint Francis, the founder of the Franciscan order. Serra became a priest in 1737 and taught philosophy in Spain. He knew that he also wanted to teach other people about the Catholic religion. So in 1749, he traveled to New Spain to work in Mexico City.

Serra worked in New Spain teaching and giving sermons until 1769, when he was chosen as president of the California missions.

He was fifty-five years old but was eager to begin converting the Native people of Alta California, so he joined Portolá's expedition to San Diego in the spring. The journey was not easy. By the time Serra and the crew arrived, half of the people in their group had died. On July 16, 1769, Fray Serra established the first mission: Mission San Diego de Alcalá. In all, Serra founded nine missions in Alta California during his lifetime.

HOW SAN ANTONIO DE PADUA BEGAN

Mission San Antonio de Padua was founded on July 14, 1771. Fray Serra, along with priests Fray Buenaventura Sitjar and Fray Miguel Pieras, several soldiers, and two neophyte families from Baja California entered an area called *Los Robles*. Spanish for "the Oaks," Los Robles is a valley located east of the California coastline in the foothills of the Santa Lucia Mountain Range. The area had fertile soil and was close to a river and many Native people from the Salinan tribes.

The story is that Fray Serra found a spot along the river and officially began Mission San Antonio by having the two friars with him hang bells on an oak tree. He rang the bells to attract the local people and called out to them to come to church. Others on the expedition told Serra that no one was around for miles (kilometers) and that no one would come. Unmoved by the comments, Serra said that he wanted to express his feelings about Christianity. And for Serra, ringing the bells held a special meaning: it was a symbol of his desire to teach everyone and let the whole world hear about the Christian religion.

Franciscans like this one ran the mission until the early twenty-first century.

The people on the expedition then constructed a temporary altar and raised a cross. Serra held the first service in Los Robles and named the mission in honor of Saint Anthony of Padua.

FRIARS AT MISSION SAN ANTONIO DE PADUA

The two friars left to care for Mission San Antonio de Padua were frays Pieras and Sitjar. Pieras began his work at the mission in 1771, when he was only thirty years old. He rarely left the grounds until he retired to New Spain in 1793.

Thirty-two-year-old Fray Sitjar was born in Majorca, Spain, in 1739. Along with Fray Pieras, he took charge of the mission in 1771. He stayed at the mission for thirty-seven years, which made him one of the longest-serving missionaries in the Alta California mission system. Fray Sitjar is credited with many accomplishments, including mastering the language spoken by the local Salinan people. He also compiled a vocabulary of Spanish explanations, which was published in New York in 1861.

5
Early Days at the Mission

RELATIONS WITH THE SALINAN GROW

After dedicating Mission San Antonio, the construction process began almost immediately. The Salinan people were friendly and offered to help build the first mission structures. These shelters were simply and quickly built. Usually young trees were used as posts and then poles were placed on top as a roof. Branches or *tule* (a kind of reed) were laid on top of the poles. Over time, the temporary structures would be rebuilt as permanent buildings.

The Salinan people were drawn to the European tools used by the missionaries, such as hammers and axes. In return for gifts of these tools, as well as clothing and food, the Salinan provided advice to the newcomers about the land. They also showed the Spanish where to find the best tule and other materials for building. At the mission, neophytes came to be known as Antoniaños.

It was easier for the missionaries of San Antonio de Padua to recruit neophytes than it was for the friars at other missions. The Native people in the areas surrounding Mission San Antonio de Padua and the Catholics shared similar ideas about gods and deities: the Salinan believed in a Creator and that life was in all things. The Salinan told the Spanish settlers that their legends were about bearded men dressed like Spaniards who had visited their land in earlier times. It is thought they were remembering the early 1600s, when Sebastián Vizcaíno visited the coast of California. The Salinan even showed the missionaries a cave full of drawings and carvings of their gods, along with what looked to be Christian crosses. This familiarity may explain why the Salinan people accepted the Catholic conversions peacefully, while other tribes were not as willing to become a part of the Christian life. The cave, painted by the Chumash and located in the Santa Barbara area, remains preserved today.

BUILDING BEGINS

The original structures were being built along the river. In 1773, a year and a half after construction began, that part of the river ran dry. There was not enough water to take care of everyone at the mission or to ensure the growth of successful crops. This was essential to the mission staying in operation. Later that year, the mission relocated about 1 mile (1.6 km) up the river, where the water supply was plentiful year round. This location was in a different part of Los Robles, at a point on the river called San Miguel Creek.

Following the move, everyone took part in the construction of a small church and a few buildings. These buildings were made of **adobe** bricks. Adobe was a mixture of mud, clay, straw, and sometimes manure. The adobe was packed into brick molds and then dried in the sun. The bricks were then covered in plaster to make them waterproof. After the plaster was applied, the bricks were

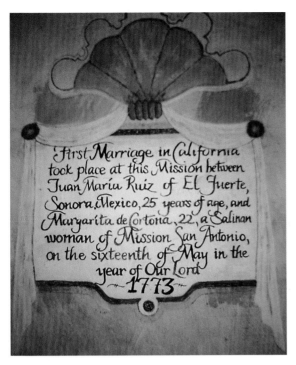

The first Catholic marriage ever recorded in California took place at Mission San Antonio de Padua.

held together with mud. The buildings were then coated with whitewash made of lime, goat's milk, and salt. The neophytes also made tiles from clay that they shaped with molds. These tiles formed the roof and were unique to Mission San Antonio de Padua structures.

At the mission, there were also a few new houses made of wood that were constructed specifically for the neophytes and soldiers. The mission was shaped like a rectangle that was centered round a courtyard. This shape is called a quadrangle. This design was used in the missions to protect against the attacks of Native tribes and also to create a close community within the mission walls. A small garden was located to the side of the courtyard. The mission also included a wine cellar with huge wine vats, an olive press used to make olive oil, and several workshops where the neophytes could practice their newly learned trades.

THE FIRST CATHOLIC WEDDING IN CALIFORNIA

Shortly after the arrival at the new mission site, the first Catholic wedding ever recorded in Alta California took place (1773). It was between a twenty-two-year-old Salinan woman named Margarita de Cortona and a twenty-five-year-old Spanish soldier named Juan Maria Ruiz.

PROBLEMS AT MISSION SAN ANTONIO

Despite the move to San Miguel, problems for the inhabitants of Mission San Antonio de Padua remained. During the spring of 1780, the wheat crop was almost destroyed by a cold frost.

To bring water to the mission, neophytes built an irrigation system made of rock pipes, like this one.

The mission neophytes used the **irrigation** system they had built to flood the fields to thaw the wheat. Everyone then prayed for nine days that the crop would be saved. That year, the crop was better than ever before. This event gave many neophytes faith in the Christian religion.

Building continued throughout almost the entire mission period. In fact, construction of the final of three mission churches—called the Grand Church—did not start until 1810 and was not completed and blessed until 1813. This long-awaited structure, which has original paintings and decorations drawn by the neophytes who lived there, remains standing today. San Antonio de Padua is now one of the largest and most accurately restored missions.

6
Life at
the Mission

A STRICT SCHEDULE

By the end of the second year, 1773, about 150 people were involved with Mission San Antonio de Padua. This was a high population for a mission in its first years. Eventually more Salinan people moved to the mission. Others lived at their own villages, but came to the mission daily for work, food, and to learn. The Salinan people were taught Catholicism and how to speak Spanish. They were also trained in European work methods, such as plowing.

The daily schedule at the mission was very strict and had to be obeyed by everyone except people who were ill. This was a very different way

Mission bells rang to signal everyone to wake, eat, work, and sleep.

of life for the neophytes. Before moving to the mission, the Salinan people were free to do what they wanted. At the mission, everyone had to work to feed, clothe, and provide for every other person. This was part of the friars' plan to make the mission a successful community. It was difficult for many Salinan people to adapt. Some did not want to surrender their personal freedoms to join the mission. Others did not realize how demanding mission life would be until it was too late and they were forced to stay.

DAILY LIFE

A typical day at Mission San Antonio de Padua was organized around the ringing of the mission bells. There were at least two bells at every mission. At Mission San Antonio they were located inside bell towers, one on either side of the main building. Throughout the day, the bells would ring at different times and have a different purpose. This included signaling people to wake or sleep, and to alert them to pray, eat, or go to work.

Days in the mission began early, around 6 a.m., with Morning Prayer. After the service, everyone at the mission came together for breakfast, which usually consisted of *atole*, or corn porridge. People were then divided to work on various projects: children went to classes with the friars to learn Spanish and listen to teachings from the Bible, and everyone else worked at their specific jobs.

The men worked in the workshops or in the fields. They grew crops of barley, corn, beans, wheat, and peas; planted fruit trees; and took care of the livestock on several ranches at the mission. The women prepared meals, made clothes, or took care of the

Friars instructed neophytes in many aspects of Spanish culture, including language, religion, and work methods.

laundry. Cooking was mainly done over an open fire. In the neophytes' village was an oven for baking bread. Some women worked at weaving and made fine blankets and cloth from cotton, wool, and flax. Others made candles or wove baskets for use at the mission. Everything used at the mission had to be made by the people who lived there, so there were jobs for everyone.

CLOTHING THE NEOPHYTES

Getting all the neophytes clothing took the missionaries a great deal of time, but it was an important part of the missionaries' attempts to "civilize" the Salinan. The Native people did not always like the idea of wearing clothes, but the missionaries insisted on this change. Men were given a blanket, a long shirt called a tunic, and a breechcloth—or loincloth—to wrap around their waists. Later, most of the men would also wear pants. Women were provided a blanket, a tunic, and a skirt.

EVENING ACTIVITIES

After the scheduled chores were completed, it was time for lunch, usually a stew of wheat, corn, or beans called *pozole*. In addition to the food that the Salinan ate with the community, every family would have a pottage—a mixture of wild seeds—that they made in their own homes. Just as they had done before living at the mission, the Native people stored these seeds in large baskets or in granaries that were kept outside. Afterwards, everyone took a *siesta,* or a rest. They then returned to work until time came for dinner and another church service. Although it conflicted with the Catholic way of life, the missionaries sometimes allowed the Antoniaños to sing their own songs and dance as they had before. This made them content living at the mission.

VISITING THEIR VILLAGES

Eventually many missionaries decided to allow the neophytes they trusted make short visits to their homes. Without these visits, many neophytes became unhappy. The friars considered these mini-vacations "necessary evils." They didn't want to let the neophytes go, but they also wanted to keep them happy. However, happiness was not always that easy. Some friars and soldiers abused the neophytes, thus some attempted to escape. They were often caught and brought back to the mission, where they were punished.

LIVING AT THE MISSION

When Native people were baptized, they were told of the mission rules that needed to be followed. These included living the lifestyle of the Spanish and becoming Spanish citizens. One way the friars ensured that the Native people would not return to their old ways was to divide families into married couples, girls, and boys. Married couples and their young children lived in small villages, called *rancherías*, a short distance from the main mission buildings. Girls eleven years or older were taken to *monjerios*—dormitories where widows and unmarried girls lived. These quarters were locked at night and guarded to ensure that no one snuck out or crept in. Young and unmarried boys also lived separately, but their buildings remained unlocked at night. They were cared for by the friars.

Before a person could join the mission, a friar had to baptize him or her into the Christian faith.

7
The Mission Declines

TIMES OF UNREST

Throughout its existence, Mission San Antonio de Padua experienced periods of unrest within the community. These events eventually led to a decline in the number of indigenous people at the mission in the mid-1800s.

The first disturbance occurred in 1775, when during a baptism, a group of non-mission Salinan began shooting arrows at the mission inhabitants. The man being baptized was wounded, but when he recovered from his injuries, some of the neophytes believed it was a sign. They thought that the mission's patron saint, Saint Anthony, had saved the baptized man. Even though the attack could have had a horrible effect on the Antoniaños' feelings about the mission, life there continued undisturbed.

During the 1800s a period of hardship began at Mission San Antonio de Padua. An epidemic of disease thought to be smallpox or measles broke out across the missions of Alta California. More neophytes were dying at the mission than were being born. The Native people had not developed immunity to the disease, thus many were affected.

Treatment of the neophytes caused other problems to surface. At some missions, they were held captive. They had to work to support the mission system and had limited choices in their daily lives. If neophytes broke the rules or ran away and were brought back, they would first be reminded that they chose to live in the mission and promised to follow the rules. If they broke the rules again, they were punished by flogging or whipping. The third time any neophyte broke the rules he or she would be forced to

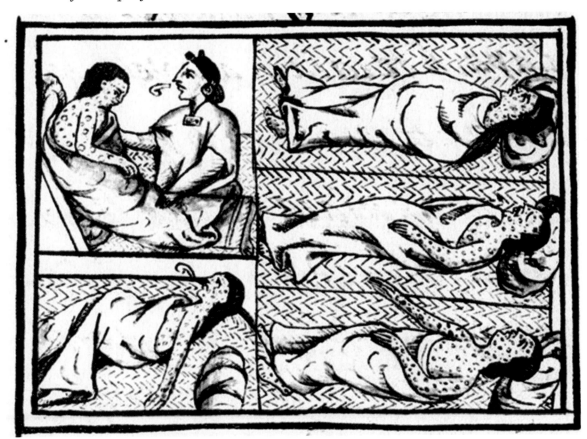

Diseases such as smallpox affected many people living in and around Mission San Antonio de Padua.

wear heavy chains while working. Women were usually punished by being held from one to three days in the **stocks**. The missionaries considered these punishments appropriate. They believed that the converted followers didn't have the same rights as everyone else.

Another problem with the mission system was that the soldiers did not always behave according to mission standards. They were tasked to uphold the rules but oftentimes broke them. There are reports of soldiers stealing from, abusing, wrongly punishing, and sometimes attacking neophytes. One reason for these problems was that the soldiers were not at the mission for the same reasons as the friars, and they did not care for the Native people. In the end, however, both soldiers and friars were held responsible for the mistreatment of the neophytes. For this reason, neophytes left and the population at Mission San Antonio greatly was reduced.

Anyone who ran away was punished when they returned—sometimes by being put in stocks similar to the one shown here.

CHANGES

In 1805, two new friars, Pedro Cabot and Juan Bautista Sancho, arrived at San Antonio to assist Fray Sitjar. They brought with them new perspectives, and Fray Sancho even taught the neophytes how to sing Gregorian chants. The mission was flourishing, but this "golden age" was short lived.

A few years later, in 1811, the people of New Spain began a revolution against the Spanish government to gain their independence. While the Spanish government was busy trying to stop rebels in Mexico, it neglected to send supplies to the missions. As a result, the mission fell on hard times, and some soldiers did not receive their pay from the government. They then stole from the neophytes and began to cause more trouble at the mission. But everything changed when, in 1821, Mexico gained its independence from Spain.

This painting of the Assumption of Mary into heaven features in Mission San Antonio de Padua today.

8
Secularization

SECULARIZATION OF THE MISSIONS

In 1821, the people of New Spain won the Mexican War of Independence (1810–1821) and formed the new nation of Mexico. Alta and Baja California became parts of Mexico. In 1833, the Mexican government passed the Secularization Act, which allowed for all the missions to be secularized, but not the way the Spanish had initially intended. Mission San Antonio de Padua was secularized in 1835.

Secularization meant that the missions, more or less, were shut down after 1834. The land was not returned to the neophytes for care. Instead a commissioner was assigned to each mission and placed in charge of managing the neophytes and their education. The friars were sent back to Spain, and Mexican priests were put on a salary and held responsible only for the religious training of the neophytes. Each male neophyte more than twenty years old was to be given 33 acres (13.4 hectares) of land. Half of the mission's tools, livestock, and seeds were also to be given to them. The idea then was that the neophytes would care for their parcels of land. However, many who took advantage of this opportunity were unprepared. Often lands were either stolen from the neophytes by con men or were handed over to private owners.

These owners eventually forbade the neophytes to be on the land. Some neophytes decided to flee the mission and live on their own. Mexican settlers then moved into the area and began ranches. Some Native people worked on these ranches and were treated badly by the Mexicans.

After 1821, Mexico gained the land that had once belonged to Spain, which included the California missions.

FALLING INTO DISREPAIR

Once the mission was returned to the Catholic Church in 1863, parts of it remained in operation by the neophytes and the last priest, Fray Doroteo Ambrís from Mexico, until his death in 1882.

After that time the mission was deserted and left to ruin. Sadly, the original tiles were stolen from the roof, and most of the walls crumbled. Mission San Antonio de Padua deteriorated more than many of the other California missions because it had fewer visitors in its remote location. From 1903 to 1908, an attempt to restore the mission was started, but only the church was restored. Much of that had to be rebuilt after the San Francisco earthquake in 1906. Through the 1950s, the Franciscans returned and continued the **restoration**, and by July 14, 1971, the San Antonio de Padua Mission was able to celebrate its two-hundredth anniversary in a partially renovated structure.

Today Mission San Antonio de Padua remains an active church, museum, and tourist attraction.

9
The Mission Today

VISITING THE MISSION TODAY

Mission San Antonio de Padua still exists today, offering visitors much to see and do. Until 2005, the Franciscans ran the mission. At that time the Franciscans handed over caretaking to the local Catholic **Diocese** of Monterey. Nestled in the grassy valley between the Santa Lucia Mountains, it remains an active Catholic parish and holds daily Masses for the community. The mission also houses a museum, where a visitor can walk into the original wine vat. Visitors can also view parts of the living quarters as they were when the mission began.

People who visit the mission today are also able to see and touch descendants of the original plant life from the mission's early days. In the center of the mission building a beautiful garden has been planted. A grapevine, grown from the seeds of an original grapevine, still grows in the garden. At the entrance to the mission is an olive tree from the 1830s, which still produces olives.

Unlike several of the other missions in California today, many artifacts from the original structures remain at Mission San Antonio de Padua. The mission's chapel houses a large number of the important original pieces of history. The original **baptistery** and **tabernacle** are located in the chapel. On the altar many of the original statues, including those of Mary and Joseph—two important figures in Christianity—are placed. When the chapel was renovated, artwork, probably from the Santa Bárbara mission, was added to the walls. Pews were also added.

Mission San Antonio de Padua's story has survived as a reminder of key moments in California's past. Just as it was the birthplace of many California "firsts," today it is a lasting monument to two different cultures and the moments that made the population of California what it is today.

Mission San Antonio de Padua will always be a gateway to California's past.

10
Make Your Own Mission Model

**To make your own model of the
San Antonio de Padua mission, you will need:**

- ruler
- scissors
- Foam Core board
- red, green, black, and terracotta paint
- Styrofoam

- cardboard
- glue
- dry lasagna
- small bell
- flowers
- trees

DIRECTIONS

**Adult supervision
is suggested.**

Step 1: Cut two church walls (front and back) measuring 7.75" × 6.75" (19.69 cm × 17.15 cm) out of Foam Core board. Paint all the sides using terracotta paint.

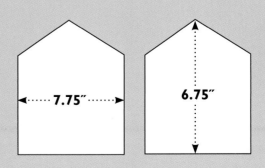

Step 2: Cut two church walls (sides) measuring 12.5" × 4.75" (31.75 cm × 12.07 cm) out of Foam Core board. Paint all sides with terracotta paint.

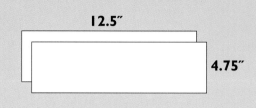

Step 3: Using the Foam Core board, cut two 12.5" × 4.75" (31.75 cm × 12.07 cm) roof panels. Paint all sides with red paint.

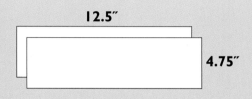

Step 4: Cut two courtyard walls (front and back) measuring 13.25" × 2.5" (33.65 cm × 6.35 cm) out of Styrofoam. Paint all sides with terracotta paint. Paint doors with black paint.

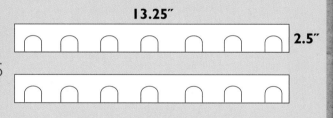

Step 5: Cut one courtyard wall (side) out of Styrofoam measuring 12.5" × 2.5" (31.75 cm × 6.35 cm). Paint all sides with terracotta paint. Paint the doors with black paint.

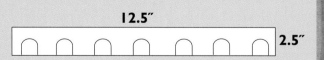

Step 6: Cut one church wall (front façade) out of Foam Core board measuring 7.75"× 2.5" (19.69 cm × 6.35 cm). Paint all sides with terracotta paint. Paint the doors with black paint. Cut a small square above the center door in which to hang the bell.

Step 7: For the base material cut a 31"× 21.5" (78.74 cm × 54.61 cm) piece of cardboard. Paint the courtyard area green. Use the terracotta paint to cover the sidewalk.

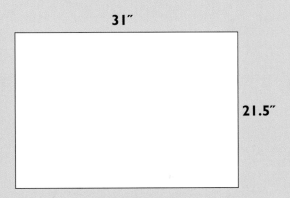

Step 8: Glue together (corner to corner) the four walls that were cut in Steps 1 and 2. Wait for the glue to dry.

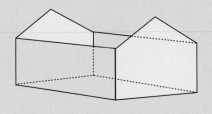

Step 9: Glue the two roof panels that were cut in Step 3 to the top of the church. Wait for the glue to dry.

Step 10: Glue the front and back courtyard walls, cut in Step 4, to the sides of the church. Wait for the glue to dry.

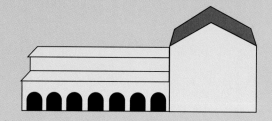

Step 11: Glue the church wall, cut in Step 5, to the front of the church structure. Wait for the glue to dry.

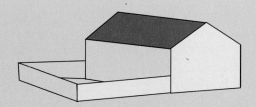

Step 12: Glue the church wall, cut in Step 6, to the front of the church structure. Wait for the glue to dry.

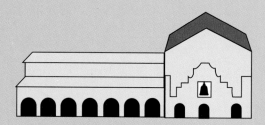

Step 13: Paint the lasagna red, and glue it to the roof panels. Wait for the glue to dry.

Step 14: Glue the entire structure to the base material that was cut in Step 7. Wait for the glue to dry.

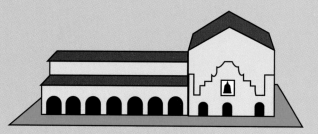

Step 15: Use a toothpick to attach the bell. Glue two toothpicks together to make a cross. Wait for the glue to dry. Glue the cross to the top front of the church. Wait for the glue to dry. Decorate the mission with flowers and trees.

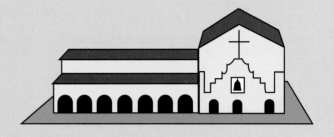

The completed model of Mission San Antonio de Padua.

Key Dates in Mission History

1492   Christopher Columbus reaches the West Indies

1542   Cabrillo's expedition to California

1602   Sebastián Vizcaíno sails to California

1713   Fray Junípero Serra is born

1769   Founding of San Diego de Alcalá

1770   Founding of San Carlos Borroméo del Río Carmelo

1771   Founding of San Antonio de Padua and San Gabriel Arcángel

1772   Founding of San Luis Obispo de Tolosa

1775–76   Founding of San Juan Capistrano

1776   Founding of San Francisco de Asís

1776   Declaration of Independence is signed

1777	Founding of Santa Clara de Asís
1782	Founding of San Buenaventura
1784	Fray Serra dies
1786	Founding of Santa Bárbara
1787	Founding of La Purísima Concepción
1791	Founding of Santa Cruz and Nuestra Señora de la Soledad
1797	Founding of San José, San Juan Bautista, San Miguel Arcángel, and San Fernando Rey de España
1798	Founding of San Luis Rey de Francia
1804	Founding of Santa Inés
1817	Founding of San Rafael Arcángel
1823	Founding of San Francisco Solano
1833	Mexico passes Secularization Act
1848	Gold found in northern California
1850	California becomes the thirty-first state

Glossary

adobe (uh-DOH-bee)
Sun-dried bricks made of straw, mud, and sometimes manure.

baptistery (BAP-tuh-stree)
Part of a church (or a separate building) used for baptisms.

Catholicism (kuh-THAH-lih-sih-zum) The faith or practice of Catholic Christianity, which includes following the spiritual leadership of priests who are headed by a pope.

Christianity (kris-chee-A-nih-tee) A religion based on the teachings of Jesus Christ and the Bible, practiced by Eastern, Roman Catholic, and Protestant groups.

conquistador (kon-KEE-stuh-dor) A person, usually a soldier, who comes to a country to take control or conquer it.

convert (kun-VERT) To change from belief in one religion to belief in another religion.

dialect (DYE-ah-lekt) An accent, or a different way of speaking a certain language.

diocese (DYE-oh-sees) A division of parish communities in the Catholic religion.

Franciscan (fran-SIS-kin) A communal Roman Catholic order of friars, or "brothers" who follow the teachings and examples of Saint Francis of Assisi, who did much work as a missionary.

friar (FRY-ur) A brother in a communal religious order. Friars can also be priests.

indigenous (in-DIH-gee-nous)
When a person, place, or thing is native to an area.

irrigation (ih-rih-GAY-shun)
A way of supplying water through artificial ditches.

neophyte (NEE-oh-fyt)
A word used to describe a Native American who recently converted to the Christian faith.

restoration (reh-stuh-RAY-shun) The process of returning something, such as a building, to its original state.

secularization (seh-kyuh-luh-rih-ZAY-shun) The process by which the missions were made to be nonreligious.

stocks (STAWKS) A wooden frame with holes in which one's feet or head and hands can be locked. Used as a type of punishment.

tabernacle (TA-ber-na-kul)
A house of worship.

viceroy (VICE-roy) A person sent by a king or queen to rule a colony in the past.

Pronunciation Guide

atole (ah-TOH-lay)

El Camino Real (EL kah-MEE-noh RAY-al)

fray (FRAY)

monjerío (mohn-hay-REE-oh)

pozole (poh-SOH-ay)

rancherías (rahn-cheh-REE-as)

Find Out More

For more information on Mission San Antonio de Padua and the California missions, check out these books and websites:

BOOKS

Brower, Pauline. *Inland Valleys Missions of California*. Minneapolis, MN: Lerner Publishing, 2008.

Duffield, Katy S. *California History for Kids*. Chicago, IL: Chicago Review Press, 2012.

Gendell, Megan. *The Spanish Missions of California*. New York, NY: Scholastic, 2010.

Gibson, Karen Bush. *Native American History for Kids*. Chicago, IL: Chicago Review Press, 2010.

Young, Stanley. *The Missions of California*. 3rd edition. San Francisco, CA: Chronicle Books, 2004.

WEBSITES

California Missions Resource Center

www.missionscalifornia.com

Interact with a mission timeline, videos, and photo gallery and unlock key facts about each mission in the California mission system.

Monterey County Historical Society

www.mchsmuseum.com/missionsant.html

Investigate the history of San Antonio de Padua and the surrounding Monterey area in this interactive and informative website.

Mission San Antonio de Padua

http://missionsanantonio.net

Explore the official web page for Mission San Antonio de Padua and learn about the mission's history and what it's like today.

For more information about Mission San Antonio de Padua, or for pamphlets, brochures, and photos distributed at the mission, contact the mission directly at:

P.O. Box 803 (End of Mission Road)
Jolon, California 93928
Phone: 831-385-4478
E-mail: office@missionsanantonio.net

Index

Page numbers in **boldface** are illustrations.